The Power Of The I Am

Julia Seton

Kessinger Publishing's Rare Reprints

Thousands of Scarce and Hard-to-Find Books on These and other Subjects!

- Americana
- Ancient Mysteries
- Animals
- Anthropology
- Architecture
- Arts
- Astrology
- Bibliographies
- Biographies & Memoirs
- Body, Mind & Spirit
- Business & Investing
- Children & Young Adult
- Collectibles
- Comparative Religions
- Crafts & Hobbies
- Earth Sciences
- Education
- Ephemera
- Fiction
- Folklore
- Geography
- Health & Diet
- History
- Hobbies & Leisure
- Humor
- Illustrated Books
- Language & Culture
- Law
- Life Sciences
- Literature
- Medicine & Pharmacy
- Metaphysical
- Music
- Mystery & Crime
- Mythology
- Natural History
- Outdoor & Nature
- Philosophy
- Poetry
- Political Science
- Science
- Psychiatry & Psychology
- Reference
- Religion & Spiritualism
- Rhetoric
- Sacred Books
- Science Fiction
- Science & Technology
- Self-Help
- Social Sciences
- Symbolism
- Theatre & Drama
- Theology
- Travel & Explorations
- War & Military
- Women
- Yoga
- *Plus Much More!*

**We kindly invite you to view our catalog list at:
http://www.kessinger.net**

THIS ARTICLE WAS EXTRACTED FROM THE BOOK:

Freedom Talks Number 1

BY THIS AUTHOR:

Julia Seton

ISBN 0766187330

READ MORE ABOUT THE BOOK AT OUR WEB SITE:

http://www.kessinger.net

OR ORDER THE COMPLETE
BOOK FROM YOUR FAVORITE STORE

ISBN 0766187330

Because this article has been extracted from a parent book, it may have non-pertinent text at the beginning or end of it.

Any blank pages following the article are necessary for our book production requirements. The article herein is complete.

THE POWER OF THE "I AM"

His Death

There was a tailor whose life seemed suddenly to be a nest of fears because he had no work. Each day he left his wife and children and went in search of work. He was bent, as tailors are bent, from sitting years upon a tailor's bench, but he walked quickly to keep up with his companion Hope.

After many days he found, one morning, a new comrade waiting for him as he went out his door. His wife saw, too, that Hope had left and that Uncertainty was there. For weeks she saw the two go out together. Uncertainty was silent, yet sometimes he flashed a smile upon his bent companion, and then he looked like Hope.

Again, one day, the tailor's wife saw still another figure waiting to go with her husband on his daily search — a brother of Uncertainty — Despair. And she cried out and begged the tailor to stay home — to wait a while until the fearful one had gone.

But the tailor passed out into the rain and walked all day as wearily as man can walk when he has searched so many months for work. And all day long

Despair clutched at his sleeve, and when the darkness came down he pushed him toward a place where drugs are sold.

That night the tailor died. His wife saw Death come in and knew Despair had brought him. The children, too, all terror-struck, began to see the visions of their mother, and they cried.

The next day thousands of the city dwellers read these words: "Yielding to despair, after a year's struggle against poverty, during which he and his family were frequently without food for days, Abraham Siegel, a tailor, ended his life in his bare room at No. 92 Henry Street. Two dollars would have saved him and would have encouraged him to further effort to find food for his suffering wife and children. He had collected three dollars to obtain a peddler's license, but the price asked was five dollars."

We could have helped him, but if we had there might have been another such as he. You, too, are, in the system which lets its work be so disorganized that men who wish to work can search in vain and then give up their life. We dare not call the system Christian, nor do we dare to call it necessary. Life costs too much to let mere want of work crush it to the depths of despair — and then to death.

CHARLOTTE TELLER.

> *"But why dost thou judge thy brother; or why dost thou set at nought thy brother; for we shall all stand before the judgment seat of Christ.*
>
> *Let us not therefore judge one another, but judge this rather, that no man put a stumbling block or occasion to fall in his brother's way: I know and am persuaded by the Lord Jesus that there is nothing unclean in itself, but to him that esteemeth any thing unclean, to him it is unclean. Have thou faith in thyself before God. Happy is he who condemneth not himself in the things which he alloweth.*
>
> *And I myself am persuaded of ye my brethren that ye also have goodness; filled with all knowledge, and able to admonish one another."*

On these verses hang the absolute truth and gospel of individuality. The strength and power, and wholeness of each life, and the absolute reign and sovereignty of the "I AM."

Individuality is the corner stone on which all humanity hangs its hopes; it is the means by which we come to turn our faces toward the light and climb from social, moral, and everlasting darkness, up toward the larger life.

The higher awakened individuality gives us a life poise which has in it the highest type of equity, and through this we recognize another's rights to be as Divinely appointed as our own.

We are asked over and over again, "What is your position toward poverty, crime, greed, selfishness and immorality? Where would you begin if you cut out reform?" You say, "Do all your reformatory stunts on yourself and let your own life prove your philosophy, and yet, you talk and lecture. What are you doing, but trying to reform people? How do you reconcile your words and your actions?"

And again we are asked, "Would you have us turn away from all of these great social, economic, and religious questions, and shutting our eyes to all human need, go on in our own little corner, as if there were no one to consider but ourselves?"

Now first as to whether New Thought attempts reform? It does not. It stands for construction; not destruction, nor reconstruction; it leaves the *old* alone; it is concerned alone with the *new*, the complete, and not with the part. Nevertheless it is true that as soon as anyone lifts his voice and says to the listening multitude, "Here; I have something to say," he immediately takes his place in the class called reformers; it is a big class, in which each one must make his own distinction.

New Thought is concerned wholly with individuals, has nothing at all to do with problems, save to prevent them; it is not concerned with the stumbling block; but it is absorbed in seeing "that no man place occasion to fall in his brother's way." It cures through prevention.

It has to do with individual position, believing that problems and conditions are the exact expression of individual creation, and that as long as individual position remains the same, expression will be bound to follow.

It sees clearly that taking care of results is the same in the social world as the treatment of symptoms in the medical world, and that both continue until the cause is found, and changed to normal. It does not advocate reform in the differentiated, but change from the center. This change can only be brought about by changing the premises from which each individual works, and from which he draws his conclusions. And this is accomplished by individual enlightenment.

The world is a stage, and the stage of life will remain the same for generations and generations yet unborn. The actors are always changing or passing on. A new play may be introduced, and new actors assume the parts, but until the world is destroyed, the stage settings will remain the same.

The north and west end of Boston, the east side of New York, and poverty stricken work folk of London will continue to exist in various degrees of expression when the last man of this generation lies dead, simply because the expressions cannot cease while the causes which project them are alive and active.

There is in every age a crowd of teachers who are working unceasingly to lift the masses into a different manifestation of life. They live, do their little life work, and pass on, and the oncoming generation find their task not completed, and they take it up and attempt new departures, and bring them to a certain point of development and they, too, go on, and the next generation opens its eyes to discover that the task is still waiting to be finished, and that the "poor ye have always with you."

There are, too, in every age, those whose eyes are open to the truth of the law of individual development; these can see the end from the beginning, and can reason from causes to effects. They know that what we call crime, poverty, sickness, wrong, is only the expression of a lower form of development of material life, and that every manifestation can be but the lawful effect of the condition which enabled it to exist. They know these expressions are on the lower darker steps of the ladder of human progress through which every soul must pass on its journey toward Good.

We all pass on that ladder, but crime and poverty need not be ultimated in physical deeds with everyone to be tangibly perceived; yet, the power to commit these crimes is possessed, on these lower planes, by all; the difference in the power of conscious willing is one of the things which controls all the conditions and makes a difference in individual expression. The criminal is not to blame that he cannot help committing crime; there are certain conditions which have obtained in his life. He says, "I cannot help it"; we say, "He will not help it," but the fact remains that he cannot will, to will, to help it, because there have been causes of sufficient power to produce them, every condition existing in his life, and these causes began back beyond the present expression of his life.

We are daily widening our concept of causes and effects. In the light of the scientific deductions of today, the expert phrenologist, aided by anatomy and physiology, can go through the wards of the state's prisons and tell to a certainty what the criminal deeds of each prisoner are. He can tell, too, if the prisoner is innocent of the crime of which he has been convicted; he tells it by the temperament of the prisoner, the formation of his brain, its development, and he brings to aid his investigation the other sciences of photophysics, graphology color examinations, and vibration.

We have many latent powers of our life's possibilities already created before anyone of us is born. A man will follow his natural instincts in defiance of everything else so long as he is unconscious or self-conscious. It is only when he can be taught to be conscious that he becomes really creative and sets himself free from the law, and wills to move to the higher level of his life.

Man runs naturally to the deeds of the human life, as the stream on its course; both may meet obstructions, and be turned away for a little while, but both are governed by unalterable laws, and tend onward toward their destination.

This nature, working with a life, is what we have and express in the self-conscious stage of development. We all have this natural life, but whether we have "life more abundant" and a "God like expression" depends upon just how carefully we study our own being and how earnestly and soon we desire to lift our personal life to the level of the Universal. The river running naturally across the miles, and carrying a diverse number of streams, may be fulfilling the law of nature, but under the control of a conscious directing power, its force is gathered into one tremendous fall, which fills a reservoir, or runs powerful machinery.

Resistance or denial never has, never can change a desire for evil into a desire for what is good; desires are natural on their own plane of existence and are a part of the unfolding plan of the life that needs them.

It would be folly to deny, that, to the limited vision, the manifestation of human life as it appears today, is wrong, but to the wider vision, the deepest convictions of consciousness, we must know that every manifestation of human life in matter, from the highest to the lowest, from the bright and beautiful to the dark and damned, is infinitely significant of good.

Man is just what he is, and will be just whatever he wants to be in spite of all human preachings and effort at restraint, and only that mighty unseen power of the latent conscious mind, within each life, has power to eventually save it.

Restraint is necessary and lawful in its place; it is true that it belongs on the same plane with crime, but it is not true that it ever cures crime. A life that needs the bridle of restraint will not be able to accept this teaching; it may need restraint a little longer; the law of its nature demands it; that life must have restraint as a resistance to evil and it is right for its condition. Such a life is all right in its present thought position but it is simply young, or immature in its development.

All human life is but a rising upward of the soul, and if there is an existing cause and agency, in every step of our Godward journey, we must come at last into that light of Divine interpretation where, if we can see the higher illumination of our life doing the holy work, we must see also the lawful cause of degradation that demands the other expression. Prison-houses, jails, churches, hospitals, asylums, have their uses and purposes and are the lawful products of the spirit of man in a certain condition of development, and in the expression of the self-conscious plane they are necessary and right.

So we can see clearly that all reforms are only a matter of position towards the changing conditions of human life, and the true reformer works because he cannot help but work, for the flower of his life has burst into bloom; he has been born again on the planes of the higher consciousness, and possesses an extended vision which sees life in its completeness.

"How do we know that we have passed from death unto life? Because we love the brethren, for he that hateth his brother is dead." The one who is so filled with love that he cannot find room within himself for any other emotion towards mankind, has passed into that big field of life where the "harvest is great but the laborers are few." The one who goes out to help his fellow man, not up, or down, but simply onward; who stands beside him with no thought of superiority, no sense of gratified ambitions, no greed, no gain, but who simply walks out into the great seething mass of mixed conditions, because he cannot help it, for the law of his life led him there; who takes each life as it touches his own, and points it to a new and better expression; who strengthens hope, lifts up the fallen, scatters joy broadcast; that man becomes indeed not a reformer, but a liberator to the imprisoned sons of God.

In the world today the people who deal with reforms, and resistance of crimes; who legislate and preach and pray, are the workers on the self-conscious plane, and are anxious about a normal expression; they are bound in a world of incidents and the futility of their work bears witness to their position.

There is a fixed law that controls the moving grains of sand and the falling comet; the same law that controls the higher spiritual, controls also the material features of the Universe, and we are forever, each day, at the judgment bar of the Infinite life, and whatever falls beneath its measure, is placed where it belongs and made manifest by those who can express it.

The general public has not even a suspicion of this differentiation of development; it is bound by the ideas of the expression of the whole, and is interested with the problem of collective human expression, and the things on the external rather than those within the individual life. We cannot hope to make our position clear to the crowd, but we do know what we can accomplish by individual awakening. Difference of development, opinion, and methods, ought not to create prejudices on either side, for it is plain that there is truth in each expression; and prejudice *does not* obtain with those who have reached the higher planes of conception where they see not only the beginning, but the end, also.

Humanity places itself in this world of human expression, and whatever we have or do not have, is but an absolute picture of just what we believed we might have, and just what we built for ourselves; no one gives to us but ourselves, no one takes away from us but ourselves; the Universal Abundance is for all; the Law is no respecter of persons, and if we are filled with lack or crime, while all around us there is an overflowing plenty, we have only to turn into our own life and seek the solution to this expression, and we will find it.

The self-conscious negative receptive unpoised creatures are living in the same world, under the same laws which obtain for the positive creative conscious successful people; and the things which they call health, happiness and prosperity, that the one half possesses and which the others do not have, exists in great abundance even while it appears to be "cornered." We may all break into this great Universal Supply Company at any moment and at any time that we have "tuned up the strong fine instrument of our being to chord with our high hope." We must know first, that we can never secure abundance while we build old poverty stricken thoughts in our whole being. The thing we want and our point of attraction must become equal, or we go on forever separated from it. We may take all the negative creatures of this world today, right now, and lift them away from their conditions by external force; we may build a new Utopia and place them in it under the most bewildering or even simple conditions of peace and power and plenty, and what will be the result; simply this, we will keep as a tribute of our grand philanthropy, a few souls which interiorly were ready for the next step onward and the great crowd of the other development will in a short time revert back to their own normal point of expression. "Ephraim is wedded to his idols," and growth comes from within, not from without. "But," some may say, "that is so only as it concerns this generation; the next one, started from that point, will be an expression of a higher energy and in a few generations there would be a grand colony of great souls." "True," but what of the other colony which would at the same time come out from the same crowd; we would find that for every ego, born in this new land, who would make union interiorly, there would be without doubt hundreds who would revert back to the original type, taking with them only slight traces of modifying influences on their life, and it would take another generation to take them on to that point in personal expression which would equal the point where they were born.

Only in those lives where the internal perception had been awakened and where the union with the higher impulses had been made, would there be the slightest desire to carry on the work which had been begun for them. Life in all its manifestations is always a sifting, and it will continue to be a sifting so long as expression continues on this plane. We pass on only as we become fit.

All so called reforms are good on their own plane, and all reformers are right in the position from which they work; but when they see only one way they become the prejudiced reformer, and do not see that only when they lift their life above the enthusiasm of the racial concept and away from the sentimental plane of the "evil and good" standard into the vibration of the brotherhood of man, and then only can they look out over a wider field where they can see this, and see the God in man developing the man God. They are then no longer reformers on the personal side of expression, but become workers in that great house of human construction, whose builder and maker is God.

When we can teach a developing life to feel and know that it is the reservoir of infinite possibilities, and that it is the "master yet of his own fate," we have given it the first and best step toward a correct position. This is life building, not reform; this is construction, not reconstruction; it is just a putting off of the old man and a putting on of the new man, and when we have a world full of teachers everywhere, who have consecrated their life to this work of uplifting, and who never speak without sending out a sound of hope and love and joy and belief in our own power of creation and our right to health, happiness and plenty, there will soon cease to be such examples as that of the tailor, whose life seemed suddenly to be a nest of fears because he had no work, and who joined his fears with uncertainty and despair and finally death. These souls will then suddenly find some one beside them who will point them to their own "I Am," and hope and joy and peace, power to secure and sense to hold, will displace the demons of the field of consciousness which are slowly becoming their judge and executioner, and they will pass on into the fullness of a new image and number one more in the great world crowd who believe in their own power as they believe in God himself.

Now, to summarize quickly, just what should be our position toward this great question of what the world pleases to call millionaires and paupers; power and lack; the over producer and the non-producer; the sweat shop and the sweated; the over-fed and the glutted aristocrats of folly; the criminal; the wretched; and also the indifferently, happy crowd? Just this, let them alone collectively, for they are only the expressions of the force which made them what they are; but, taking each one, and as many as touch our life, telling them the truth about their relation to *universal abundance* and human rights as we see it, and whenever we find an answering response in a life, by helping it to reach its highest point of conception and expression. Do not make laws and try to torture and hang or force the thousands we cannot reach, into what we conceive to be Truth. It is not always possible to determine for another just what is needed for the correct development of a life. When we have spoken the Truth, as we see it, and in every way and in every hour and by every word which we know, we can let them alone; our work is ended; "God is in his Heaven and all is well with the world."

The teachers, leaders, healers and ministers all have this one Divine mission to perform; they need only "to go about their Father's business and do always these things which pleaseth the Father." Christ said the "poor ye have always with ye," and again, "as ye did it unto the least of these, ye did it unto me."

We have only to sow the seeds of consciousness and the truth of the uplifting of the "I Am" within every human life until it faces around and makes some sort of union with the Infinite Life, so that from the shores of the Absolute wisdom great waves of Truth may beat in upon it; we have then done our life-work. We sow the seed; it does not matter where it falls. We all know the story of the sower; how some of the seed fell by the wayside, some fell on the rocks to die, but others fell deep into fertile soil and brought forth a harvest.

So I say again, not reform but "life building" is our watchword. We are all in different stages of unfoldment; some are the green fruit, some the buds, some the blossoms and others the ripened fruit, and our position is the expression of our growth.

Let those of us who feel that they *know*, and who have the torch of intense throbbing human love alight within their breast, go out into the dank miasma ladened thought-swamps of the self-conscious world, and carry with them a new song of hope, peace, plenty, power and Divine realization; let us take with us the message of the greatness of the "I Am." The voice said to Moses "say only 'I Am that I Am.'" Let those who teach, say it again and again; say it to all who listen; say in it love and power and sweetness until it falls like a benediction upon a faltering life, and it turns toward the hope of a new endeavor, and says, "Lord I believe. Help Thou my unbelief."

When we teach the downcast hearts to know and feel their divine relationship; that their expression may become perfect, beautiful and whole, we give them a courage so majestic, that in the midst of their greatest failures they walk on, serene and calm, with a grand strength which in time conquers all things.

As we go on in this higher leading, inspiring and building, great crowds of lives will be sifted out from each generation, until at last, "persisting, and perfecting in endeavor, we yet may bring forth *angels* after men."

This is the end of this publication.

Any remaining blank pages are for our book binding requirements and are blank on purpose.

To search thousands of interesting publications like this one, please remember to visit our website at:

http://www.kessinger.net